First Edition October 2020

Paperback ISBN: 9798694603706
eBook ISBN-13: 9781234567890
eBook ISBN-10: 1477123456

Cover Artwork and Interior Illustrations by:
Daniela Coronado (IG: @writinggibsongirl)
Library of Congress Control Number: 2018675309
Printed in the United States of America

The following selection was published prior to this publication:
"Juniper Churchbell" in *Brushfire #58*.

eshleighton.com

BACKWARDS BIRTHS

poems

ESH LEIGHTON

to my William, my light and sound
I promise to listen to more jazz if you'll read more poetry

BACKWARDS BIRTHS

Contents

★

Contents - Continued

PART NIGHT: WINGED THING

The Nevadan

Take me back to the desert.

I'm tired of the condensation that pools
and drips from the ceiling down my collar
down the back of my shirt like a boy sticking a wet finger where it
doesn't belong
I don't want to die in California
with her mountains and her ocean
The people,
they are born, they live, and they die singing, "California!
California!"
bathing in her waters and drinking her wine
She's not mine

Take me back to the desert.

California fights me
her crumbling coastlines
her deep rooted trees
I wonder, could I drive past the tree
that killed Jolyn?
Would it stand proud
indignant or
indifferent
for taking the life of the long time
Californian
Does its bark bear a scar
Does the winter air flow any differently through its branches,
blowing the past away with the fog

Take me back to the desert.

The acrid air smells like cigarettes and
ozone
I could die with dust in my mouth, remembering California,
and all her people
therein

Goodbye

I know
our language is mutable
malleable
and wont to change
ever evolving
but I'm an old soul
and I like
the version I was given
at birth.
When my little pink tongue learned to speak,
it liked the version it inherited
and didn't wish to change it.

I know
that when my grandchild's
grandchild's
grandchild
reads this
it will be archaic.
The words lost to the wind of time,
eroded.
And they won't know
what the fuck I am saying.
(Will they still recognize my expletive?
I hope so.)

God be with ye,
words of time.
God be with ye.

Hospital Rooms and Hallways

There's a phone ringing in a bright hallway
and my husband's panicking on the floor
"That's not my mother," he says to me
his eyes wild and unfocused
He's not seeing me
He sees the thing that consumed his mother
though she is tucked away in a room around the corner

He held it together until we got to the
bank of elevators
but now, he's lost it
Whatever semblance of control
he had, gone gone
He has passed that torch to me

It's wrong, you see
The thing that gave birth to him is being
drained dry by something else
something sinister and sticky and black
Tar in her lungs and a mass on her brain
She looked frail and frightened and
only a little familiar

But
"That's not my mother."
I'll hear it like the tolling of a bell for years
Tinnitus of his words echoing and echoing
I wear so much of his pain
I weave it into a sweater a cape a quilt
and wrap myself in it and carry it with me
So many folds of terror in his eyes
of sadness of grief of pain
I swallow them whole and never digest them

They'll sit inside me like a bezoar
One day someone will crack me open and find
the weight of someone else's world
all tucked up inside me
all folded around me
spilling out my mouth and eyes and ears
It's the only way to get him off the floor

Mourning Glory

If I die,
alone in a bed,
mine or hospital or hospice
after eighty good years
or a hundred
or a hundred and two,
will people tell my family,
"You were lucky to have had her this long"

?

What of me
Will I be lucky to have had myself
this long
Will I tire of these eyes
all their brown burdens
the blurred memories they bestow
their mass in my head
their moss-covered irises

Will my limbs fail me
or my lungs
or my loins

What of Death
Will he take my name
on his tongue like a communion wafer
and tell me,
"You almost had it right"

?

No.

I'll wake
to darkness
and with a tongue of dust
and a mind composed
of naught but wind
I'll greet the night
and think,
Good morning, glory

Yesterday's Poets

You whisper from graves
You riot in death
You may have gone
but not quietly
as your words still rumble
like thunder
over barren lands
and tumble
through time
to make a home
in my ears.

I will carry your torch,
my darlings.
I'll light up the world
and demand
better.

Down the Hatch
(Song of My Sister)

The thing that swallowed her,
swallowed her not whole
but bit by bit.
Incrementally.
There was less of her every day
until there was none left at all.

Sometimes I think
I can hear her calling
from down its throat,
crying for help or
laughing like she used to.
But it's only my imagination.
It's only a figment of
my memory.

She's gone
and all I'm left with
is the thing that swallowed her.
This mean and ugly thing.
It's hungry with nothing left to eat.
It gnaws at my ankles and
my back.
I feed it nothing.
It shrieks
indignantly
and it sounds like
her.

Night is a Winged Thing

I look at pictures of owls
their wings spread out against a blue-black sky
I'm not brave enough to find them
in the darkness
I'll be sated by digital evidence
that they, too, exist
and I am not alone in the night

Birds in my lenses
raptors on my screen
a winged world beyond me
I access from the comfort of my bed

I tell them each,
beautiful thing:
you are why humans dream of hunting
why we long for wings
why we know the smell of sunsets
and the rush of air beneath us,
though we will never learn to fly

Ashes, Ashes

Where have you gone, my darling?
I search in fog and
behind lightning.
but but
I cannot find you;
you must be hiding.

Where have you gone, my heart?
I comb through brush and
under dark.
but but
I lost you somewhere,
your bite, your bark.

I found your little shadow
just before you left
she came down the river
harbinger of your death.

I cannot fucking find you
I let you get away.
I let you fall through my fingers I let you slide
I let you go I let you go away.

I wish you'd stay.

All Wild and Forgotten
(Anthem of Artists)

this is what we do
this is what we do in the night
we creep from sewers
up from drains
we scratch our claws down trees
and walk down quiet streets
like smudges on old film
like apparitions
like Death, himself

to bring
to bring to you
our lovely black hearts
on platters
on forks
in Halloween pumpkins
bleeding our blackness
our long-lost love
bleeding it for you
so you might drink
and swallow
and remember

Pomme de Terre

The French translation
for potato
is
"apple of the earth"

I think of this often
in cemeteries

We are but apples
in wooden boxes
our big beautiful brains
our fat fingers
our closed eyes

They are seeds
for the world

We are fruit
ripe for the picking

Legions of apples
buried in the earth

Undisturbed and
growing, growing

I brought seeds to the cemetery
in lieu of flowers

I thought the ground deserved
something better
something with potential

A Photograph of Allie in Brooklyn

When Allie died
it made missing New York
hurt a little less
how can I mourn a city
when a piece of my soul
has died?

But they both still catch me

I'll muster in my head 14th St.
or The Village
or that little theater in Cobble Hill
and the loss will wash over me
the smell of the city on a summer night
something warm and delicious with an underpinning of
garbage and cigarette smoke and old oil
like how dissonant chords played on piano keys
in the right progression feel satisfying in your ears
New York is fucking jazz

I'll think of Al's big black nose
or her whine
or her velvet ears
I'll think of that spot just behind the pad of her paws
that my thumb would fit into like a worry stone
and I'll be lost in dismay
how can there be a world without her?
She was a better person than
any human
and she was a fucking dog

I'll remember
I had something great once
though it feels far off and foreign
like something I dreamed years ago
it left a flavor in my mouth
a color in my mind
music in my bones

I have a photograph of Allie
on the street somewhere in Brooklyn
red bricks behind her
her eyes wide
mouth agape
like she, too, couldn't believe
she was lucky enough to live there

I am the Morning, I am the Night

Here is a morning, bruised and blue
Here is a person
She's little and true
She dips her toes into the pool
Like testing out love on somebody new.

Here is a noon, beaming and golden
Here is our girl
And the love she is holding
She holds it tightly, warm and bespoken
Like an owl to her breast, not yet beholden.

Here is a dusk, fragrant and heady
Here is the woman
Grown full and ready
She's round and rotund with love in her belly
She's filled to the brim and oh-so unsteady.

Here is the night, purple and magic
Here is our crone
Speaking death, speaking tragic
She breathes into the eve, like a wind wreaking havoc,
"Goodnight men, goodnight systems, goodnight static."

Here is the midnight, black as pitch
Here are the ashes,
The remains of the witch
But here is the moment,
Gone in a twitch.
Here is your midnight and
Here is the switch.

PART DUSK:
WET GRAVITY

Calliope

I planted flowers in my womb
It seemed like a good idea,
to capitalize on space
to maximize
what wasn't being used

I'll store all my ideas
all my fervor
all my poetry
deep in the recesses of my little
pink pocket

Someday I'll birth my
magnum opus
and people will say,
"Imagine a world where she had stayed home
and was a housewife, instead?"

Fugue State

I don't know what comes over
me.
There were blank white spaces
and now there is art.

There were.
Glowing and boring
banal but clean
a universe of possibility
a world of improbability.

There are
words to fill your voids.
Thoughts you had but did not speak.
I proffer them to you
like little white cakes on silver trays
for you to taste and remark upon.

"Feminist art"
"Poetess"
"Wordsmith"
"I don't get it."
"Does anyone read anymore?"

It doesn't matter.
I wrote them not for you
or you
but for you.
(*you*)
I wrote them in another state
three thousand miles away
a hundred leagues deep

for *you* to find
on *your* fishing expeditions
your deep sea adventures
to bring onto *your* boat
to carve into their gilled flesh
when *you* have the time
and digest them
all your own.

The Fruit and Its Juices

You sit in the other room
your big bare feet arched at the toe
sorting through stacks of vinyl
bits of our income pressed into wax

as I eat a peach, too ripe,
over the sink
and let the juice run
down my fingers

I get to the pit and think
I'll plant it in the yard
and maybe it'll take root
and grow and yield summer fruit

We won't be in this house
anymore, the fruit and
its juices destined for the mouth of
someone else

but a piece of me will remain
a thing that touched my lips
and tongue and mouth
some of me will remain

You always say to me,
"If the juice is worth the squeeze…"
It was me you pressed and

my juices you found worthy
of all the crushing
I, in turn, put you through
tell me

twelve years in
are my peaches overripe
do you still find me
calling to you for a good

squeeze

The Mouth of the River

I'm going back to Louisiana
where they sow their magic
like seeds
where they light it on fire
and tuck it in their lanterns to illuminate the
night

they set it adrift on the delta
and feed it to the river
a sacrifice to the water
come from fire
and sown of earth

Flowers All the Way Down

Our fingers glide past ourselves
We are told
we are wilting flowers on the vine
soft petals, pink and pollinated
or ripened fruit
or single white pearls at
the mouth of an oyster

I am no man's flower
I am an ocean unto myself
waves parting and crashing
ushering in life and death
scented wild and honest
like when the tide
is full and pregnant
gaping at the moon
undulating beneath the sky and knowing
I'm what makes it blue

I Know Its Name

I've seen the sad

I've observed its shape,
rolled up on itself like a tube of toothpaste,
cradling its own head and humming like a bird

I've smelled it on the wind
the scent of burning things and cedar,
flooding my nose with warm decay on cool nights

I've watched it bleed
in coppery puddles and red virtue
leaking life through nostrils and tear ducts

I've held it close and felt its shape,
big and bloated and fighting against me
and losing and losing and losing

I've heard its cries
howling like a faraway beast,
moaning like something dying slowly, slowly

I know its color,
bruised and purple, a night sky without stars,
ink and paint and charcoal and dust

I have seen the sad
and I know its taste
It's here, on our many pink tongues,
it has a name
and it's here, among us

The Synesthesiac and The Original Man

Blue barbarian man
I have never seen you so angry
I swear I wasn't trying to push you away
     (Away.
      Away with you.)
as you capitulate to your temper
in a riotous rage of blue flames
so hot, they burn you from the inside out
which is why you exhale smoke in
enormous clouds that envelope our house
and rain little black flags of ash down on
     everything
I am covered in the soot from your lungs
and the remnants of your demons

I would apologize, but it wouldn't change your color

Prayer for the Crone

My knees are stained
as if by tea leaves
from kneeling in the dirty ground
from praying to a dirty god.

What vision did my knees divine?
They will not knock or kneel
any longer.

The Revisionist

I've seen your shadow, it's long as a dress
And it covers us, smothers them, cloisters
Some.

You walk through the wet streets of a city
So old, it clings to its secrets like the dirt
Beneath your hardened nails. You man.
Hey, you man. Human. We all bleed red
Inside and sleep in the night but you, Man:
You think this human experience is yours,
And yours alone. You think the blood,
Breath, and mornings are your something
Special.

You keep your city with its revisionist
History. You keep your mouth gaping and
Teeth scraping at the taste of your lies.
You keep your clothes dry, your socks
Warm and woolen in your boots because
If you admitted it was raining, you'd
Have to buy the whole damn world an
Umbrella.

The Marriage Mirage

I.
We are not little.
We are enormous.
I had a vision of us as
two halves of a planet
snowcapped mountains
and
green things growing on our valley floor.
We are whole and sublime in our enormity.
Little moons fall into our orbit
as we spin, spin into
oblivion.

II.
I am a red room
warm and replete
with splendor
warm and complete
within myself.
But don't you make a fine guest
as you sit upon my chair
and lie upon my carpet
as you sup at my table
and spill your dinner on the floor.

This Old Garden
(Or Another Just Like It)

A midday sleep.
Your arm draped over me
leaves a damp stripe on my torso.
Sunlight pours in,
bouncing off the red roof tiles
of the house next door.
I know what they sound like.
Like terra cotta pots scraping
against one another.

In another world
where you and I never met,
where you only drank coffee
at the shop where I worked
the old barn converted,
the big brass eagle atop the espresso machine
covered in dust and webs.
Did you notice me then
the girl behind the counter
I'm always the girl behind the counter.

We'd go to our deaths
having only basal interactions
and would never have had this life we built,
tangled together like the birds in my tattoo
every interaction a just and coupled action.
You push, I pull
We push, we pull

No.
You'd spiral off into your own separate oblivion
never having had more than a cup of coffee.

We'd surrender to sleep
after the long days that were
our lives,
none the wiser that we once
scraped by each other
like terra cotta pots
in an old garden.

Flies at the Mouth of a (Sacred) Cow

While I was busy
getting married
(my mouth and lips tied
to another)
you were publishing
words
about men who hurt you
men who put themselves
where you never invited
them to go

I was marrying my
man
inviting his hands
and ring
finger
into my voids.

You were fighting
men
as you swatted their
hands
away like flies.

They gave you paper
to spill your words onto
like your own honey colored
blood.

And I let my paper
fly away
on the winds
of my own pale
breath.

Childless on a Sunday Evening

Her words catch me.
    She says,
    "Perhaps the most selfless act
    she can do as a mother
    is never to become one."

Her words catch in my bones
like foxtails in fur.

I think of the little pink sons
I'll never birth
their indignant howls echoing through hospital rooms,
confused by freshly bestowed light and life.

I think of the tiny hands of daughters
I'll never hold
impatiently tugging tugging tugging
prying my attention away
to redirect it to themselves.

I'll never hear *Mommy*.
I feel this in my blood and breath.

I think of my bear of a husband,
his great big hands perfect for holding
tiny bodies,
and his childish enthusiasm,
and his patience
buried in the ground and
gone to rot
never bestowed upon
the beautiful children we won't have.

I mourn from temple to toe
a legacy of dirt and dust.

How do I give this world to a child?
How do I ask an infant to swallow this
burning blue marble
this waterlogged thing, this scorched thing
Good luck, baby,
you didn't want air to breathe, did you?

My babies would have been sharp
and funny
and gorgeous little beasts.

I mourn.

And my womb will remain taught
and fraught
with the memory
of the fantasy
of what it is to grow a world
within.

Thermodynamics

I am perfect
under the shirt you toss away
over my naked, baked body

I feel your warmth
soft in cotton
the entropy of your bones
and blood
and muscles
working to make you
to build you
to break you

Your cells,
your energy
caught in cotton
and thrown over me

like a blanket
full
of your soul

A House (Well Lived In)

Outside
I hear the water running
like a hungry stomach
Soon, soon
this house will be
a home

A cat on the sill
dogs on the hearth
and
the million little germs we bring with us

When are you coming home?
I miss your footfalls
and
your noise

Remember our first house
the bougainvillea in the garden
and
the skylight over the shower
We watched the presidential inauguration
from bed
I read 1984 on the patio
and
we fucked on the counter

Now
there are empty halls
and
blank walls
I need to fight with you
over where to hang
our artwork

You always want it higher because
you're so goddamned tall

I painted a picture of you
years ago
a likeness our guests proclaimed
uncanny
It's just your outline
your hair and beard
your lips and jaw
We're older now
and
it doesn't resemble you
anymore

When is he coming home?
I ask the empty walls
and
our many dogs
They don't answer
or
they don't know
Time ebbs like a lung
In day out night
and
a house isn't a home
without you

Swallows

I only swim in the ocean on calm days
It frightens me
The riptides and the enormity
The breakers and the waves
But you

You are enormous
And I fit you
Your breakers, your waves
I swallow them whole
You
I swallow you whole

Here, In this Imagined Space

I build things
They are as much for you
as they are for me

I gather sticks from the garden
and honey
and words you forgot you'd spoken

I craft them into something grand
their backbones, brilliant
their spines of splendor

Their flesh is your laughter
it bubbles from your mouth
and coats their lonely bones

Their soul is the memories
of favorite meals
enjoyed on warm city nights

Their blood is our blood
we bleed for this marriage
in car wrecks and headers over handlebars

And these are our children
the only ones we'll ever have
they line our cupboards and hide in cabinets

I'll take them into old age
and hope they are enough to keep me company
and to remind me to remember

This is our life
the depth and girth and breadth
these lonely sculptures

and all the spaces in between

PART NOON:
MOUTHFUL OF DIRT,
HANDFUL OF BEES

The Great Writer's Block in the Sky

I was a black hole
that fell asleep
and missed the opportunity
to absorb everything
around it for a while

I closed my eyes

Planets
Stars
Symposiums
Cacophonies
They floated by my dormant
self
and nothing was turned to nothing

Crooked Little Thing

Oh, sweet body.
You, of the tilted uterus
You, of the curved spine
You, of the red, red arm
You, of the giant fingers
      (but only two and only on one SIDE)
      (localized gigantISM)
That left breast bigger
      (they say that's for the heart)
That left foot larger
Left leg longer
Left hip lower
It's all right.
      (the right has its share, too)
      (that's where the port wine bl e e d s)
      (my wholly original birthmark archipelagos;
      when I was little, I imagined the people who populated my
      continents. Would they love each other? Would they war?
      Would they proclaim me their God?)
      (God of the People of the Free Nations of Hemangioma)
Oh, crooked teeth
Oh, lips
Oh, fingernails
Oh, freckles
Oh, fuck.
I forgive you for this slight Dutch-angled view;
you give the world cinematic glory.

Slow Trains

We rumbled and swayed
through tunnels
under rivers
past dark and dripping walls
like backwards births

You leaned into me and fell asleep
your big black (and gray) head a
mass of ash
like an aging crow on my shoulder
We called the R train
"The Rarely"
because it rarely came

And

Laughing with old friends
in a new city,
the oldest city we'd known
but full of novelty and promise
and European attitude
that made it newly hatched to us
like a wet bird wriggling in its shell

And

Angry
so fucking angry with each other
but throwing it in hoarse whispers
because
this isn't solo transport
we weren't
players in a whisper theatre

And now

Can a train carry us back
from the desert?
Can it find us and burrow(borough)
its way underground
under New Mexico and Texas
under Missour-a and Ill-annoyed

Rock and rumble and sway
us,
the only passengers,
brought back from whence we came
on a slow, slow train
back to the city that stole my soul

The Bartender
(Counting Money in the Dark)

A neon poet
A Sunday warrior
I learned to be a person
in twenty-four hour towns
These mountains and
these hills shaped me as much
as the spirits
I pour.

Spirits

Every time I pour
a spirit
do I give away some of mine?
1.5 ounces—
let's be frank—
2 ounces at a time?
No one ever accused me
of having a light hand.
Perhaps I should have garnered
a little bit of myself
before pouring her all away.

Myself

Losing pieces
little pieces like
watching marbles spill out
on a hardwood floor.
They gather in corners
and under furniture
and are lost
in the nooks
of the world.

It's Only a Satellite
(The Rift)

There's a big fat moon
on the edge
on the edge of your
spoon
and it's gonna fall
and it's gonna break us
it'll splash into the ocean
and break us in twain

and we'll be two
like twins on mountains
with the earth and the moon
and the ocean betwixt us

and we'll wave
and wave
in big warm sweaters
to our twin on the mountain
wishing for better
better weather
like our twin in the sweater
who has it
who's got it
who's got better weather

Pink Holes and Lullabies

Razor sharp teeth, she excuses
Herself and takes a phone call in
The hall. Annie had sinned once.
Annie and all the rest. The walls
Are pink but not sweet. Not jovial
But old and tired and full of secrets.
"Hello?" Hello. Hell, Oh. You're incon-
Sequential. The dinner is fucked anyway.
They don't like you. They see through
Your banter and your cinnamon. You're
Callow. You're hollow. Annie, excuse
Yourself and find your sweater and
Head out into the night. There are street
Lights to pray to, all amber and smooth
As honey, like when you were little. Like
When you were sick and bruised pink
And tried to sweeten your tea but ended
Up down on the ground with a mouthful of
Dirt and a handful of bees and no honey.
None at all.

Ode to The Tongue

I am broken
but still can taste

I lick all the fragile
little
beads of sweat

where they gather on your chest
and

taste a savory troubadour man
on this
my tongue
which is ripe from
the lashings
and

the salt

Origami in Reverse

I am a tiny fleck
a scrap of paper
trying to unfold myself
into something grand
and noticeable
like a rolling white flag
like a constitution
like birth
(legs spreading,
life cresting)

"Please
take this and
see me,"
I say like a merchant
passing flyers out by hand
little bits of myself
end up litter
down 3rd Avenue
all my hard work
all myself
caught under park benches
and dampened
in gutters.

Priscilla's Millennial Pink

he comes in the night and
Whispers, "Priscilla, Priscilla…"
In that hoarse way
Like there are rocks in his throat
he smells of smoke and tangerines
As he shoves his hands down
Down

he doesn't clean his
Guitar strings
The fretboard smudged
From dirty fingers
he wants things only when
he wants them
Women and music
he uses them
Balls them up
And throws them
Away

he's an L.A. man,
Through and through
his mother named him
Something clever
And there's honey in his pockets
And money on his floor
Though his apartment's cheap
And seedy

You know this
You find him irritating
And yet
You let yourself forget
When he comes into your room
And moans in your ear,
"Priscilla, Priscilla…"
his hands gone
Down
Lost inside

Möbius Strip

There was a little hole into your world
a window a mirror a fissure
and through it I could see your whole self
your breasts pushed up in a fancy pink bra
your round face and shoulders
your freckles your big blue eyes
and every day you opened the hole bigger
pushed more of yourself against its edges
let the edges cut into you and

Bleed
You
Dry

Let them impale you and expose
you your innards your organs your sick
and the little hole became the whole world
all of our freckles our insecurities
our breasts pushed up in fancy pink bras
we danced around, bleeding and begging
for the world's attention
while the world was preoccupied begging for ours

They Call Him November

you are
an enigma
of salt and
pouting mouth
insolence and
rib bones

you are rife
with haste
and self
regression

you are
broken and
shake like a
jar of pennies

you taste
of sand and
apples

they climb
into your
eyes and
come out
brown

Captions Written Beneath Digital Photographic Evidence of a Life Lived in Hills and Valleys, Cities and Cities

I.
The morning robs me
of pride and farce and façade
I am the wilting vine

II.
All this life
waiting on conductors
of trains
trains of thought
my mind is the caboose

III.
The mirror is a cunt,
it tells salty lies
I try not to listen,
it gives the stink eye

IV.
My soul, like my skin,
warm and freckled
left out to dry
in the noonday sun
I shrug it on like
an old familiar sweater
sometimes, it smells of you

V.
I'm growing older
and so are you
Time and time and time
She knocks on the door, repeatedly,
like a great gust of wind
One day, she'll break through

The Prodigal Generation

All of my friends are beautiful alcoholics.
We have terrible trouble with the melancholic.
Such a shame.
The collective voice of silent masturbation is
the collective despair of the sentient generation.

I am alone.

I am Odysseus. I am Ophelia.

We like the taste of whiskey
but abhor the taste of gin.
Let's try forgiveness.
Let's try for sin.

All these pretty lights look a bit like
teeth in angry mouths.
The mouths of lushes. The mouths of babes...
         (I could write an ode to the ellipses)

I am Ophelia. I am Ulysses.
I am Elizabeth. I am Odysseus.

All of our vigor comes from cocaine.
We are the very existence; we are the misery and
the bane.
What a waste.
Shh...
         Cynical sinners, this is your one infatuation.
The silent violence is your self-suffocation.

I am awake.

I am the larynx. I am the Sphinx.

We like the idea of touch
but despise the sensation.
A world of tasting tongues,
a world of pure imagination.

Your pretty teeth look a bit like
moths beating me to the flame.
The flame, the fire, the ember.
In a world of burning books,
we are the paper.
      (I owe everything to parentheses)

I am the fountain pen. I am the dying bees.
I am the teakettle. I am the thief.

PART MORNING: THE YOUNG KING

Wanton (Wanting)

I want

> to sleep beneath your grandmother's knitted blanket and
> feel the air conditioning pass through the yarn

I want

> to bake a cake in a big Bundt pan, the recipe written in my
> mother's hand and

I want

> to feed it to you in bed and let the crumbs gather in the
> sheets and have immediate OCD urges and change the
> bedsheets to new, fresh ones, the gray ones that feel silky
> on our skin

I want

> to make a child, and I want it to grow to be smart and
> insightful and someone all its own and nothing like me,
> nothing like me at all

I want

> to write a thousand pages and leave a legacy of paper and
> ink and ink and paper

I want

> you to make love to me, tenderly or turbulently, just like
> the ocean that flexes and bends and makes love to the shore

I want

> to run until my muscles burn and my legs collapse under
> me and

I want

> to feel the concrete scrape against my skin, pale and pliable

I want

> to paint something abstract, or learn to paint something concrete

I want

> to read every volume of my favorite writers, all at once like gorging on too big a meal

I want

> to swim in the ocean but only as long as the water is warm and the waves are calm

I want

> to buy you a piano and make small talk with the men who deliver it on a weekday afternoon

I want

> to cut off my hair, to shave it down to a buzz and feel the summer wind on my scalp and my neck

I want

> to get a tattoo of a lamppost in the night

I want

> to get on a plane and ask it, gently, not to crash

I want

> to rip out my uterus and let it shrivel into dust

I want

> to bury my things; I don't need them anymore

I want

> to burn things: paper, photos, scraps of a life long lived

I want
> to create

I want
> to destroy

I want
> to search

I want
> to yearn

I want
> to live

I want
> to lie

I want
> to want

I want
> to want

A Red Ripe

I have buttoned it up
locked it away
No warm slices of bread
baking on a hearth
No one walking into the room
like a babe bursting from
a red, ripe cunt

My voice in my head
carries age like spoilage
She says ancient things I don't comprehend
like she's made of candlesticks and oil,
chifforobe and cobwebs

I will never be a mother
I will turn into
that old crow in my head
She of black lace and long shadows
She of the night

But once,
I was hatched
I was hatched, once
Not of onyx
Not speaking with yesterday's cadence

I was little and fresh and
bursting forward
like walking into a room
Like bread baked fresh
Like open windows and doors ajar
letting in a soft morning wind

Wood that I Were

Would that I were
in a gentle wood
mushrooms slowly cresting
the rotting soil beneath me
earthy
yearning
growing like moss like lichen
a soft wind stirring
the leaves in the trees
like a hearty soup
the aroma just as supple
and somewhere, somewhere
snow begins to fall

But
I'm here
in an air-conditioned room
surrounded by plastic
and woven cotton
in a manufactured house
with hollow doors
and windows, shut tight
waiting for Thoreau
waiting
waiting
waiting for it to snow

Buy Used, Very Good Condition

When was I ever new?
I've felt these wheels and these sirens
these arteries and this mind
turning over and over
for a hundred fucking years.

When I was young,
        (No, when was I young? Was it ever?
        What a strange word: Ever. I am ever.
        Ever waiting ever failing.
        Ever broken ever falling)
I was not patient.
I have never been patient.

I was born used, old, and worrisome
a child Atlas with the weight
of the world and the wait
for my body to catch up to my soul.
Just a grandmother in toddler shoes.

I am ever.
I am ever.

Things I Feed My Lonely Heart
(The Trajectory of My Life Can Be Illustrated Thusly)

I. Autumn apples baked with butter, cinnamon, and cardamom

II. Scraps of paper lit by match to burn in the sulfury haze that catches in your nose; or, the ashes of nag champa incense left unattended

III. Antique turquoise, pulled from silver jewelry and ground into a coarse, blue dust

IV. Semen, which sounds lewd but has from time to time sustained when I had nothing else

V. The dog hair that catches in my throat like wet nests in which spring birds might use to lay their eggs

VI. Soot colored snow, packed tightly and nearly melted, stored in the corners of Manhattan (and the outer boroughs)

VII. Tea: black and sweetened with 2% milk and sweet-n-low; or Earl Gray with honey, soy, and vanilla; or oolong and one sugar because I need less sweetness as I age

Child of Sagan

"I am a child of
the moon,"
she proclaims
for she is stupid
and doesn't realize
we're all children of
the moon
and sun.

The moon makes the tides
makes water dance
makes the creatures inside submerged
want to crawl for the shore.

We're all stardust
recycled
recirculated
worked back through the
digestive system that is time.

We're all from one atom
(one Adam?
the bible got lost in the homonyms)
one point smaller than small
simpler than simple
basic as basic as basic
can be.

"I am a moonchild."
I say the same
because I, too, am stupid.
Basic as basic as basic
can be.
Child of the moon
and sun.
Child of the moonchild.

Still, I Dreamt of You
(Mother Ocean)

I still dream of you
your winds stilled
your wings inert
your waves calm

(or sometimes twelve miles high)

But you carry me and
cradle me
in big blue arms
you open your blouse to me
and underneath
there is calm, quiet,
answers in your depths

I find myself beneath your surface
I dream of sand and sea life
of little archipelagos I have to
hop between to reach
boats stranded in the water
boats big enough for me
and me alone
lest I capsize

(and sometimes I do)

And though I know you

you're not blue
you're volatile
you're unwelcoming
I still dream of you
as if you'll change
for my wanting
it to be so

I Was Never Taught to Run

I.

This is all I am
this sinew and fat and bone
I take it and move it
to and fro
I move it like I should've
long, long ago

It feels like Jupiter
It feels like Jupiter, falling away

II.

Somewhere, she'll break
she'll split in two
one half propelled forward
racing for the morning
hoping she gains enough speed
to spin the world back on its axis

The other half shed like old skin
crumpled in a heap
of discarded emotion
no form
just colors and feelings
and the weight
of an epitaph for yesterday

She doesn't need both, now
She never really did

III.

I am faster than my mother

Cerebellum

When I was young
and I was the king,
there was a tolling in my head
like great mallets banging on
my brass crown

and I thought it
music.

I'm not old
but I'm older
and the tolling is
calling,
>   "Come back to
>   the beginning
>   and your kingdom
>   and your reckless lust for
>   life,"
it says.

It rings
like so many tawdry
bells
like so many drunken
fools
like innocence
like wakefulness
like fat brown eyes full of water, blinking to break the dam.

It sings
like a chorus of muses
waiting for their king.

Feels So Real

When I was a child
I birthed plastic babes

The little pink hands of
my baby-feels-so-real
digging into my back
hiding beneath my body
my sister's hands on my knees
as she told me to push
she pulled the baby from under me
I grunted and sighed
tired from pretending
and she plopped the doll on my belly
for that first skin-on-plastic contact

I nursed the babe
from a chest with no breast
imaginary milk to sustain
the little polymer thing
I pushed on her head
she had a soft spot
just like a real baby
molded on an infant-sized
skeleton
cast in a cavity
for mass production

I am a woman
full grown and no
no baby
no more milk in my breast
than when I was five

I grunt and sigh
so tired from pretending
that there is a trajectory
to this life
when in reality
we live lives pre-molded
some with babies
and some with memories
of mass-produced motherhood

Juniper Churchbell

By the juniper tree,
the potent smell of berries and
death plagues
what lamb slept
here.

Momma made rice for dinner
last night,
with something spicy for
Daddy's palate.
And she'd make lamb tonight,

if only my little friend hadn't died.
Next to
the juniper tree,
its roots twisting like a rope
for the noose

for the baby.
Passed into the night
(or is it light?)
like a silent church bell
tolling not in brass, not in

metal at all,
but in the low murmur
of wooden crying.
In the low murmur
of my ardent heart.

Little lamb had so
much to carry.
His skin loose
like
he was dressed
in his brother's borrowed clothes
or hand-me-downs.

Lay me down
by my little friend.
Wayfarer in the
San Bernardinos
on his way to juniper resurrection,

for lambs tend to rise away from
their tired, broken bodies.
Momma said that's a lie.
Blasphemy.
No afterlife for lambs
and

their mortal souls.
But if my lamb,
my freckle-nosed lamb,
is meant for the earth
not

the angels,
not
rebirth
then I wish to die
beside him

and be murdered
in the silence
of the night

or the cacophony
of the dawn

or the canopy of shade
cast by the juniper tree,
and be forever hushed
and still like a stone
beside him.

Acknowledgements

★

I would like to thank the following people in helping me with the journey of birthing *Backwards Births*. Charlotte Zang, Alex Knudsen, Madeleine Elizabeth, and Gabriella Rivera for being early readers and for providing such varied suggestions and unabashed praise. I value each of you, immensely.

To my illustrator, Daniela Coronado, a veritable ray of sunshine. I am so grateful for you. Thank you for understanding what I wanted and for embodying the spirit of these works with your creations.

Thank you to my husband, William, for putting up with my cranky writer moods and always offering to brew me coffee, for marveling at my vocabulary and never once making me feel like the little woman. You'll forever be my man-muse.

Specific and special thanks to my momma, my OG first reader of everything, my biggest champion, she whom I inherited all my poetry from. Thank you for always bugging me to read what I'm penning; your excitement is contagious. I promise to write more.

And finally, thank you to you, the reader who holds these words in your hand. The world of poetry is a vast sea any poet can get lost on. Each of you is a lighthouse in a storm.